THINGS YOU SHOULD KNOW ABOUT

BUGS

By Steve Parker
Illustrated by Richard Draper

Miles Kelly
PUBLISHING

First published in 2004 by
Miles Kelly Publishing Ltd
Bardfield Centre
Great Bardfield
Essex, CM7 4SL

10 9 8 7 6 5 4 3 2 1

Editorial Director: Anne Marshall
Project Editor: Belinda Gallagher
Editorial Assistant: Lisa Clayden
Designer: HERRING BONE DESIGN
Artwork Commissioning: Bethany Walker
Production: Estela Godoy
Indexer: Jane Parker

ISBN 1-84236-196-1

Printed in China

www.mileskelly.net
info@mileskelly.net

British Library Cataloguing-in-Publication Data
A catalogue record for this book is available
from the British Library

Contents

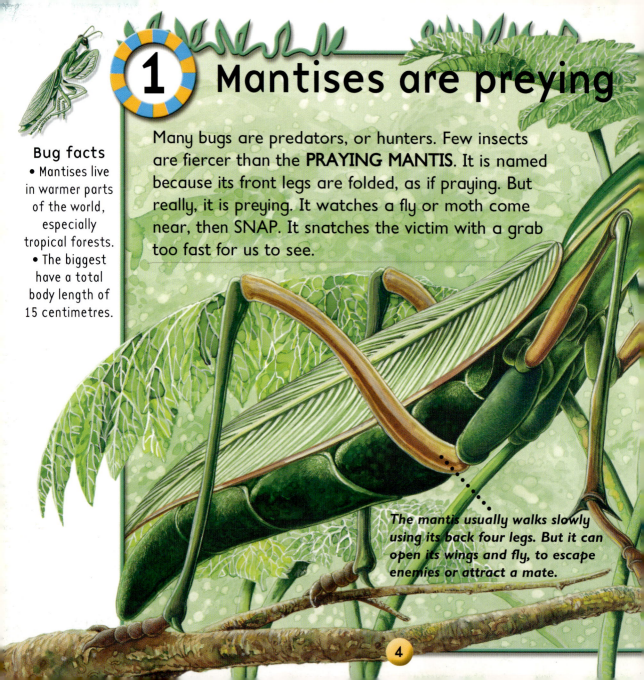

1 Mantises are preying

Bug facts
• Mantises live in warmer parts of the world, especially tropical forests.
• The biggest have a total body length of 15 centimetres.

Many bugs are predators, or hunters. Few insects are fiercer than the **PRAYING MANTIS**. It is named because its front legs are folded, as if praying. But really, it is preying. It watches a fly or moth come near, then SNAP. It snatches the victim with a grab too fast for us to see.

The mantis usually walks slowly using its back four legs. But it can open its wings and fly, to escape enemies or attract a mate.

The mantis has massive eyes and hunts mainly by sight Sometimes it may creep up on prey, but usually it snatches the meal out of mid air.

The mantis's green colour blends with the leaves around it. Even its eyes match! Its prey does not notice any danger until it is too late.

The front legs fold back on themselves to stick their sharp spines into a victim. The mantis's 'jaws' move from side to side. They chop and tear up the meal, usually starting with the head!

Mantis wings!

Most insects have wings. They are usually folded over the back, but are used to fly the insect from danger.

Bees do not mind dying

Bug facts
• A big honey bee nest has more than 50,000 worker bees, who are all sisters.
• Only one, the queen bee, lays eggs. She is larger than all the others.

HONEY BEES are social insects. This means they live in a group, or colony, in a nest. They share jobs such as finding food, cleaning the nest and caring for the young. In fact, they will even die for each other so that the whole colony can survive.

Some bees forage outside, searching for sweet flower nectar. Then they return to the nest and 'dance' to tell other bees where the flowers are.

Flower power!

As bees collect pollen, they spread it from flower to flower, to make new seeds. With fewer bees, there would be fewer flowers.

The bee's sting is at its rear end. If it jabs the sting into an enemy, the back part of its body is torn off, and the bee is certain to die.

A nest has hundreds of six-sided cells with wax walls. Here, young bees hatch into grubs.

Some cells contain stored food the bees have made from nectar and pollen – this is honey.

3 Monarchs fly long-distance!

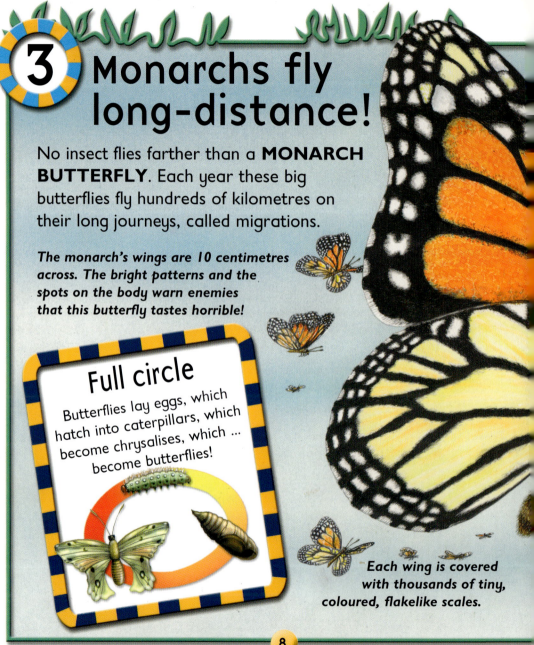

No insect flies farther than a **MONARCH BUTTERFLY**. Each year these big butterflies fly hundreds of kilometres on their long journeys, called migrations.

The monarch's wings are 10 centimetres across. The bright patterns and the spots on the body warn enemies that this butterfly tastes horrible!

Bug facts

• After a winter rest, monarchs fly north in the spring – they stop to breed, then they die.

• Monarchs are also called milkweed butterflies, as their caterpillars feed only on this plant.

• Monarch caterpillars are about 5 centimetres in length.

Full circle

Butterflies lay eggs, which hatch into caterpillars, which become chrysalises, which ... become butterflies!

Each wing is covered with thousands of tiny, coloured, flakelike scales.

The butterfly senses wind and air currents with its long antennae (feelers). These also 'smell' the air for scents of flowers.

Monarchs can fly an amazing 2000 kilometres on migration, covering 150 kilometres in a single day!

The two wings on each side are joined by a tiny hook. This allows both the front and back wings to flap as one.

The monarch's 'tongue' is shaped like a coiled-up drinking straw. It unrolls to sip the flower's juices and nectar.

4 Locusts love leaves!

Bug facts
- The biggest locust swarms have measured more than 50 kilometres in length.
- They contained more than 250 billion locusts.

Desert **LOCUSTS** are a type of grasshopper. They live in dry, remote areas. But sometimes, when rains come and plants grow quickly, locusts feed well and breed well. Then they feed more and breed more. Soon there are millions of them, and they take to the air in a huge, hungry cloud.

Locusts live in all warm places. The biggest swarms are found in Africa.

A giant swarm of locusts darkens the sky for hours as it flies in search of food.

If locusts find a field of crops, they swoop down and begin to feast. The whole field can be gone in less than an hour.

As locusts feed, they crawl or hop from plant to plant. They use their long, strong back legs to leap away from danger.

In one day, a single locust can fly 20 kilometres and then eat its own weight in food – mainly plant leaves, stems, shoots and buds.

Hopping mad!
When locusts hatch, they are wingless hoppers. They have to jump between meals.

5 Beetles can be kings

Bug facts
- The great diving beetle grows to 5 centimetres in length.
- Various kinds of diving beetles live in ponds all over the world.

A pond is like a mini-jungle, where the **GREAT DIVING BEETLE** is king of the hunters. It is fast and fierce, with large, fanglike jaws to seize and stab victims such as tadpoles, worms and baby fish. No small creature is safe from this thumb-sized underwater terror!

The beetle hunts using its big eyes. Its antennae (feelers) detect ripples in the water caused by escaping prey.

The victim is grabbed by pincer-like feet on the beetle's front legs, then pulled towards its long, sharp jaws.

The great diving beetle comes to the surface to trap bubbles of air under the wing-cases on its back. It breathes this stored air while underwater.

This is a female great diving beetle – she has grooves, or furrows, along the wing-cases on her back. The male's back is smooth and shiny.

The bristly legs work like paddles to row through the water.

A tasty meal

Diving beetles quickly catch prey that fall into the pond – from flies to worms.

6 Army ants march on

Bug facts

- Some colonies of army ants in South America have more than one million 'soldiers'.
- Similar ants, called driver ants, live in African forests.

ARMY ANTS march in long lines across the tropical forest floor, left right three times (with their six legs), until they feel hungry. Then they stop. Some gather round to set up a simple nest for a few days. Others set out to find food – and kill any creature they find.

The ants crowd around a victim, bite and sting it, then chop it into tiny pieces with their strong 'jaws'.

Pieces of food are taken back to the rest of the colony, in the nest.

14

Any animal that cannot escape is attacked by the ants. They can strip the meat off a wild pig in four hours. Even the giant anteater runs away from army ants!

Giant queen

Only a queen ant lays eggs. She is huge, five times bigger than a guard, which is twice as big as a worker.

Small groups called scouting parties search for more food.

Moths like moonlight

The **MOON MOTH** flits like a ghost through the night sky. Most moths like the light of the moon as they search for plant juices such as nectar in flowers. By day they rest in cracks in rocks or among leaves. Butterflies prefer to fly during the day.

Moths have antennae (feelers) shaped like feathers. At breeding time the male moth uses his antennae to smell the scent of the female from 5 kilometres away.

Bug facts

• Moon moths are large, with wings 15 centimetres across.

• Atlas moths are even bigger – with wings almost 30 centimetres across they are the largest flying insects.

Make a moth
Fold some paper in half. Open it up and paint moth wings on one side. Fold again and press down. Open up to see all of the moth!

The moon moth's long 'tails' are mainly for show, to attract a partner. The two 'dance' in the moonlight. By day, as the moth rests, the tails look like old, curled-up leaves.

The wide wings have large spots, like staring eyes. At a quick glance, this makes the moth look like a big-eyed owl, which scares away enemies.

17

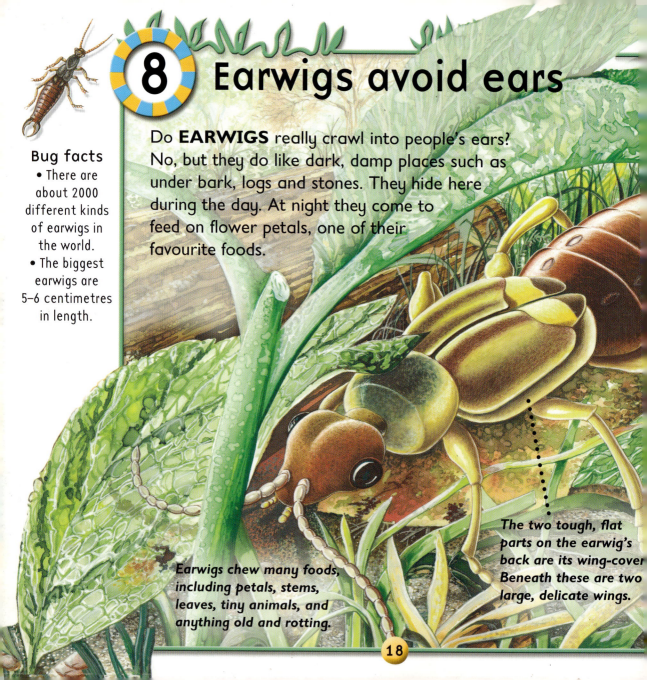

8 Earwigs avoid ears

Do **EARWIGS** really crawl into people's ears? No, but they do like dark, damp places such as under bark, logs and stones. They hide here during the day. At night they come to feed on flower petals, one of their favourite foods.

Bug facts
- There are about 2000 different kinds of earwigs in the world.
- The biggest earwigs are 5–6 centimetres in length.

Earwigs chew many foods, including petals, stems, leaves, tiny animals, and anything old and rotting.

The two tough, flat parts on the earwig's back are its wing-cover Beneath these are two large, delicate wings.

The tail pincers are used to fold up the wings after flying. The earwig also holds its partner by the tail pincers when breeding.

The female earwig has almost straight pincers. The male's are more curved, like a C.

Earwigs have a low, flat body. They can crawl into a narrow opening to hide from enemies, such as spiders, frogs and birds.

Mother-wig

A mother earwig takes good care of her eggs. She cleans and protects them.

9 Dragonflies have bug-eyes!

Bug facts

- In ancient times, before dinosaurs, lived huge dragonflies with wings 60 centimetres across.
- Today's dragonflies are smaller. But they are still big for insects, with wingspans of up to 20 centimetres.

DRAGONFLIES have huge eyes. They take up over half the head. Expert hunters, dragonflies have a sharp mouth for cutting up their meals.

Water baby

A young dragonfly, called a nymph, lacks wings and it lives in a pond! But it is just as fierce at hunting as its parents.

The wings make a whirring noise as they beat up and down ten times every second.

This is a hawker dragonfly. It has a long, slim body and swoops to and fro over the same area near a pond or river.

Darter dragonflies have shorter, fatter bodies. They sit on a perch and dart out when they spot a meal flying by.

When it has found a meal, the dragonfly returns to its perch. There it begins to bite the victim into pieces, to eat the softer parts.

The dragonfly's eye is made of many tiny parts. Each one sees a small area of the view. A dragonfly has more of these parts than any other bug, more than 30,000 in each eye!

The ground under the dragonfly's perch is covered with legs, wings and other bits from its meal that were too tough to eat.

Dragonflies catch their food with their legs. They hold out the front legs like a 'basket' to scoop up flies, gnats and moths.

Bugs can bring death

Bug facts

• The disease malaria is spread by a type of mosquito called the anopheles. It kills nearly 3 million people each year.

• Other diseases spread by flies, fleas, lice and other bugs kill more than 50 million people each year.

Many insects spread germs and disease. The **MOSQUITO** is one of the deadliest. In hotter parts of the world, when it bites people to suck their blood, it may pass on a terrible illness such as malaria or yellow fever.

To a tiny mosquito, the hairs on our skin are huge, almost like flagpoles! First the mosquito searches for where the skin is thin, such as near the wrist or ankle.

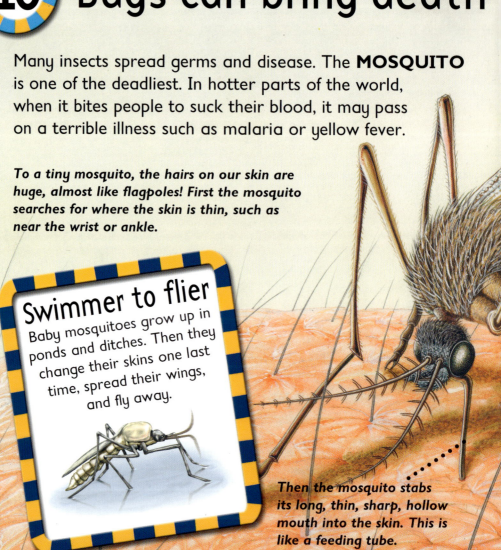

Swimmer to flier

Baby mosquitoes grow up in ponds and ditches. Then they change their skins one last time, spread their wings, and fly away.

Then the mosquito stabs its long, thin, sharp, hollow mouth into the skin. This is like a feeding tube.

Next the mosquito sucks up blood through its tubelike mouth.

As the mosquito sucks, its body swells up like a warm, red balloon. Then the mosquito slides out its feeding tube and buzzes off, before the person realizes what has happened.

It is usually female mosquitoes that feed on blood. They use its nutrients to make their eggs. Most male mosquitoes are not blood-suckers. They feed on flowers, plants and moulds.

Index